P9-DGK-054

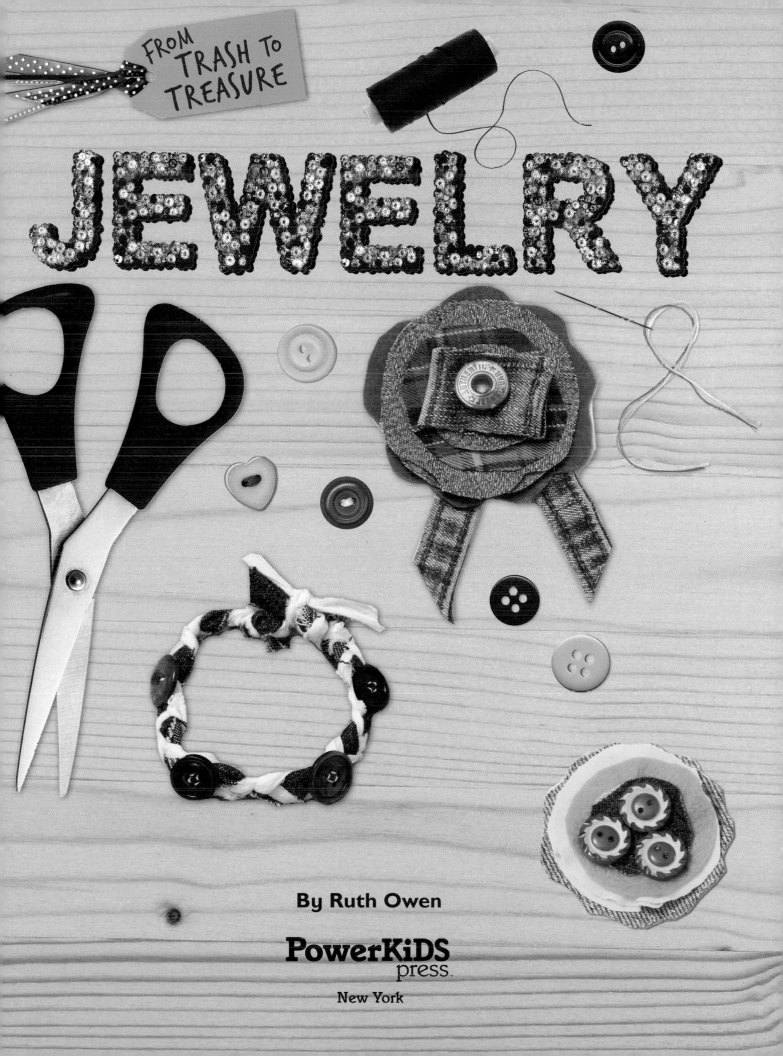

FROM TRASH TO TREASURE

JEWELRY

By Ruth Owen

PowerKiDS press.

New York

Published in 2014 by The Rosen Publishing Group, Inc.
29 East 21st Street, New York, NY 10010

First Edition

Produced for Rosen by Ruby Tuesday Books Ltd
Editor for Ruby Tuesday Books Ltd: Mark J. Sachner
US Editor: Joshua Shadowens
Designer: Emma Randall

Photo Credits:
Cover, 1, 3, 4 (bottom), 5, 6 (right), 10 (left), 14, 17 (bottom), 18 (left), 22 © Shutterstock; cover, 1, 4–5 (center), 6 (left), 7, 8–9, 10 (right), 11, 12–13, 15, 16, 17 (top), 18 (right), 19, 20–21, 23, 24–25, 26–27, 28–29, 30–31 © Ruth Owen and John Such.

Library of Congress Cataloging-in-Publication Data

Owen, Ruth, 1967–
Jewelry / by Ruth Owen. — First edition.
    pages cm. — (From trash to treasure)
Includes index.
ISBN 978-1-4777-1283-2 (library binding) — ISBN 978-1-4777-1360-0 (paperback) — ISBN 978-1-4777-1361-7 (6-pack)
1. Handicraft—Juvenile literature. 2. Jewelry making—Juvenile literature. 3. Recycling (Waste, etc.)—Juvenile literature. I. Title.
TT171.O94 2014
745.594'2—dc23
                          2013011125

Manufactured in the United States of America

CPSIA Compliance Information: Batch #S13PK8: For Further Information contact Rosen Publishing, New York, New York at 1-800-237-9932

CONTENTS

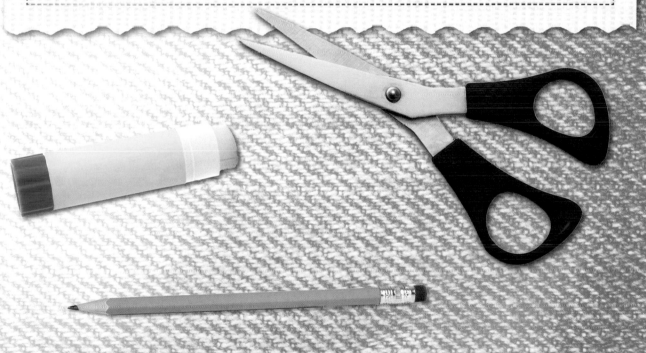

TRASH TO DESIGNER TREASURE

Every year, we throw away paper, packaging materials, plastic containers, glass bottles and jars, clothes, shoes, and many other items.

Many of these trash items can be **recycled**. They are collected from our homes and taken to recycling facilities. There, the materials are turned back into **raw materials** that are used to make new plastic containers, glass bottles, and other items.

In addition to recycling trash, some people look for ways to reuse it and turn it into something new. Today, many jewelry designers create beautiful pieces of **costume jewelry** from recycled glass, paper, and even old clothes. But guess what? You don't have to be a professional jewelry maker to design and make recycled jewelry. Get creating today, and turn your family's trash into treasure.

The average American will throw away about 90,000 pounds (40,800 kg) of trash in his or her lifetime. Are you sure there's nothing in that garbage bag that could be reused?

4

This necklace has been made from old rings. The cute recycled denim purse was made from a pair of old jeans!

Recycled paper is used to make paper towels, notebooks, envelopes, printer paper, boxes, compost for growing plants in, and even kitty litter. Some jewelry designers use paper from magazines and newspapers to make paper beads.

RAG FRIENDSHIP BRACELETS

About 5 percent of the trash that ends up in **landfills** around the United States consists of clothes and footwear. Sometimes these clothes are too old or damaged to be reused. However, many items could be recycled.

Unwanted clothes that can still be worn may be given to thrift shops. These stores are run by **charities**, and the items are sold for just a few dollars to help raise money to pay for the charity's work. These shops also give people an inexpensive place to buy clothes of their own.

You can recycle clothes this way, or you can use old, damaged, or unwanted clothes to make **unique** pieces of recycled jewelry, such as these cute rag friendship bracelets.

You will need:
- Any fabric that is thin enough to tear, especially if it will fray slightly
- Scissors
- Small shirt buttons
- A needle and thread

STEP 1:
Cut or tear three strips of fabric. The strips should be less than one inch (2.5 cm) thick and 12 inches (30 cm) long. The strips can be the same color or a mixture of colors.

If you tear the strips and allow the fabric to fray a little, it gives a nice ragged edge that works for the look of this bracelet.

STEP 2:
Tie the three strips together at one end. You can do this by tying one strip around the other two in a double knot.

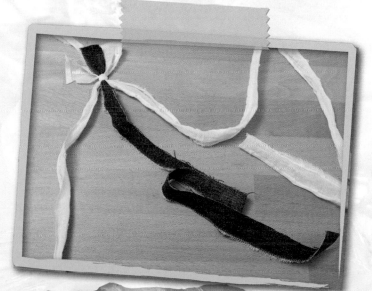

STEP 3:
Now braid the strips together.

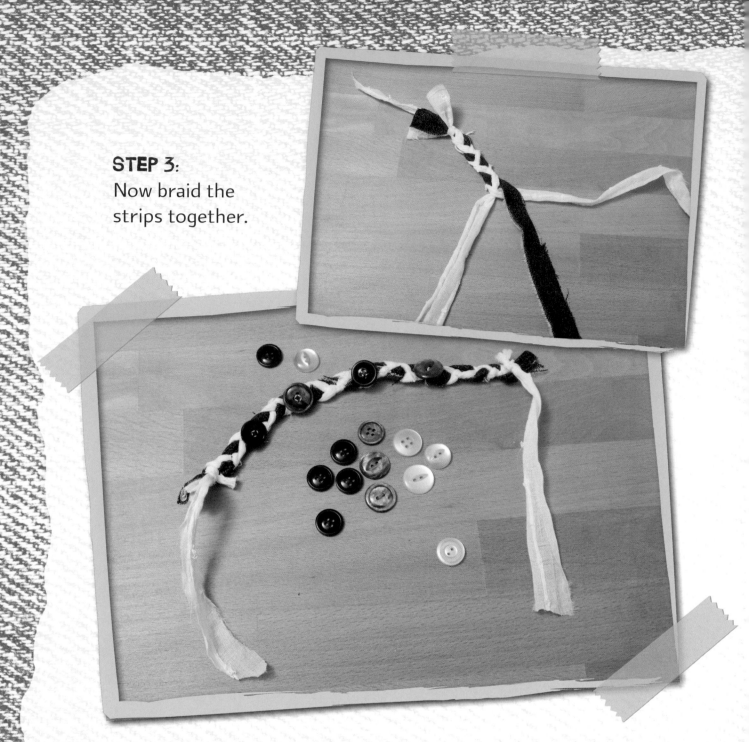

STEP 4:
Once you've made a braid long enough to go around your wrist, tie up the strips so the braid doesn't unravel. Trim off any excess fabric.

STEP 5:
Now tie a thin strip of fabric about 3 to 4 inches (7.5–10 cm) long to each end of the bracelet. These two strips can be tied in a knot and bow to secure the bracelet around your wrist.

STEP 6:

Stitch small shirt buttons onto the bracelet as a decoration, and your simple rag bracelet is ready to wear!

RUBBER BAND JEWELRY

Rubber bands are extremely useful for keeping food containers tightly closed or for holding hair in a braid or ponytail.

Sometimes, however, you end up with quite a few of these stretchy little rings lurking in drawers and knickknack bowls around the house. You could wrap them around each other to make a rubber band ball. Or you could use them to make some funky, colorful, long-lasting, and even waterproof costume jewelry. Collect rubber bands from your home, and ask friends and family to donate to your recycled rubber band collection. Then get started stringing the bands together.

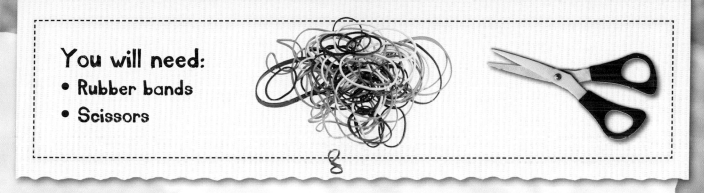

STEP 1:

The design of this rubber band jewelry is based on a chain. Each section of the rubber band chain is made up of three rubber bands. So begin by sorting your bands into groups of three.

STEP 2:

Cut through an extra rubber band to use as a stretchy piece of string. Then take one group of three bands and tie them around the middle with the piece of rubber string.

STEP 3:

You will now have a loop on each side of the knotted string. Take another three rubber bands and thread them through the two loops and pull everything tight. You've now made one section of the chain.

STEP 4:

Now, continue to loop sets of three rubber bands through each other.

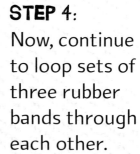

STEP 5:

Keep adding sections until you have a chain the length you want. Then take the final group of three rubber bands, loop the piece of stretchy string through them, and tie the end section to the first section of the chain. Trim off the ends of the string.

Tie the end section to the first section with the stretchy string.

You can make necklaces, bracelets, belts, and even straps for purses using this rubber band chain design. Make pieces of jewelry in single colors or try out different color combos.

FABRIC SCRAP BROOCHES

Handmade brooches often sell in designer boutiques. You can make your own unique brooches, though, by **upcycling** old badges and buttons and decorating them with recycled fabric scraps.

These brooches are not only fun to make, but they are quick, too. Maybe you could start your own **environmentally friendly** jewelry business making and selling recycled brooches to your friends and family. You can turn trash into spending money or even donate some of your **profits** to a **conservation organization**. Your creativity could help fund the work of people who are helping protect wildlife and the **environment**.

Volunteer

VOTE

Old buttons or badges

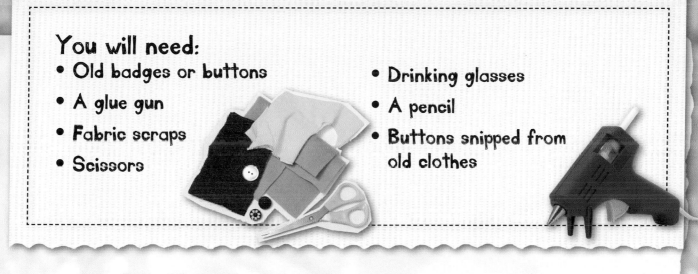

You will need:

- Old badges or buttons
- A glue gun
- Fabric scraps
- Scissors
- Drinking glasses
- A pencil
- Buttons snipped from old clothes

STEP 1:

For each brooch, cut four or five small circles of fabric. The circles should get smaller and smaller and be in contrasting or alternating colors.

STEP 2:

You can cut the circles freehand, as it doesn't matter if they have a slightly rough edge. Or turn a glass upside-down on the fabric and draw around the glass to get a perfect circle. Use glasses in different sizes to get different-sized circles.

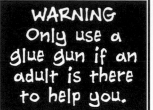

STEP 3:

Take the largest circle and squeeze some glue into its center. Take the next size circle and press it into the glue. Slightly pleat and scrunch this circle to give the brooch a 3D or raised effect.

STEP 4:

Build up the layers of your brooch by gluing on smaller and smaller circles. Then glue on some buttons.

STEP 5:

Finally, squeeze glue onto an old badge and then press your finished fabric brooch onto the sticky surface of the badge.

If you wish, you can give the bottom layer of fabric a curvy edge to look like the shape of a flower.

Make different designs using fabric from old clothes, felt scraps from other craft projects, and even lace. Be as creative as you want!

OLD T-SHIRT NECKLACE

A cotton T-shirt may be a cheap piece of clothing to buy, but its cost to the environment can be high.

Growing the cotton needed to make one T-shirt can require 700 gallons (2,650 l) of water. When T-shirts are made in factories in China, wastewater containing the chemicals used to dye the T-shirts different colors sometimes ends up in rivers, harming wildlife and **polluting** people's drinking water.

So try to find out the environmental impact of your clothing before you buy. And then make sure, when your T-shirt is too raggedy to wear, it doesn't end up in a landfill, but gets reused. For example, you can recycle your T-shirt as a chunky, braided necklace made from strips of T-shirt fabric.

How green is your T-shirt?

You will need:
- Two old T-shirts in contrasting colors
- Scissors
- Beads
- A needle and thread

STEP 1:
Starting at the bottom hem of a T-shirt, cut off a strip that's about 1 inch (2.5 cm) wide and about 24 inches (60 cm) long.

STEP 2:
Keep cutting until you've turned the body of the T-shirt into strips.

Repeat with another T-shirt that's a contrasting color.

STEP 3:
Gently pull on the strips of fabric to stretch them, and they will curl up and look like thick yarn.

STEP 4:
Take three strips and tie them together.

STEP 5:
Now braid the strips together.

STEP 6:
Once you've made a braid long enough for a necklace that will slide over your head, tie up the strands so the braid doesn't unravel.

STEP 7:
Then tie the two ends of the necklace together. You can join the two ends by tying a strand from each end together into a double knot. Trim off the excess fabric, or leave a chunky bunch of knots and short strands to be a pendant-like part of the necklace.

STEP 8:
Stitch some big, chunky beads onto the necklace. Use beads from a craft store, or recycle beads from a broken or old, unwanted necklace. Add the beads in a repetitive pattern, stitch them on randomly, or position them all in one bunch.

JEAN POCKET PURSE

When your favorite jeans are too shabby to wear any longer, you can turn them into something new, such as a cute little purse!

It's the environmentally friendly thing to do, because a lot of water, electricity, and fuel went into making that one piece of clothing. Gallons (l) of water were used to grow the cotton to make the denim. Fuel was used to transport the cotton to a fabric mill, where water and electricity were used to turn it into denim. The fabric then traveled to a factory, where more energy was used to make the fabric into jeans. Finally, the jeans may have traveled thousands of miles (km) from the factory to the store where you bought them.

Cotton (the white fluffy stuff) is grown on farms as a crop.

You will need:
- An old pair of jeans
- Scissors
- A needle and thread
- Fabric scraps and buttons for decoration
- A glue gun

STEP 1:
Cut a section from the back of the jeans that contains a pocket, and cut off one leg of the jeans.

STEP 2:
Cut the pocket from the jeans. You can either cut tight to the hems of the pocket, or leave a little excess fabric that will fray and add to the funky, recycled look of the purse.

Excess fabric that can be pulled to make it fray and give it a tattered look.

23

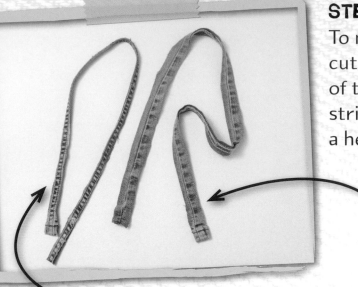

STEP 3:

To make a long strap for the bag, cut a strip of fabric from the leg of the jeans. You can either cut a strip of plain fabric or incorporate a hem into your design.

1-inch- (2.5-cm-) thick strip of denim incorporating a hem

Thin strip of hem just using the double thickness part of the hem

STEP 4:

Now decorate the purse with small scraps of denim. The jeans we used had a tiny pocket on the front that we cut off to use as a decoration.

Fabric scrap flower

Small pocket

STEP 5:

Trim circles of denim and mix them up with other fabric scraps to make a decorative flower for the front of the bag. (See fabric scrap brooch instructions on page 14.) We finished off our flower with the button from the jeans.

STEP 6:
Stitch each end of the strap to the back of the purse.

STEP 7:
Glue or stitch your decorations to the front of the purse. Be careful to only stitch to the front of the purse and not all the way through to the back!

MINI JEWELRY BOX

Plastic containers are part of our everyday lives. From soda bottles to yogurt cartons, shampoo bottles to jars of face cream.

If you're reading this book, you probably already recycle every plastic container that you can. When that plastic reaches a recycling facility, it is sorted according to the type of plastic. Then it is washed and ground into small flakes. The flakes are then dried, melted, and made into pellets, or small lumps, of plastic. These pellets are then sent to factories to become the raw material to make new plastic containers.

In this project, you can recycle a plastic face cream container and turn it into a completely new type of container: a beautiful beaded mini jewelry box!

You will need:

- A plastic face cream container with a lid
- Fabric scraps
- A pencil
- Scissors
- A glue gun
- Beads from old, broken necklaces, or buttons from recycled items of clothing

STEP 1:

Find an empty face cream or body lotion container with a lid, and wash it thoroughly.

STEP 2:

Place the base of the container upside-down on the fabric and draw around it.

STEP 3:

Cut out the fabric circle and then glue it inside the container to give a soft base to the jewelry box. Be careful not to get hot glue on your fingers when using the glue gun.

WARNING
Only use a glue gun if an adult is there to help you.

STEP 4:

Now place the lid onto a piece of fabric. Draw a circle that's big enough to cover the lid of the container and its sides. The circle doesn't have to be perfect. Cut out the circle.

STEP 5:

Squeeze glue over the top of the lid, then press it into the center of the circle you've just cut out. Then cover about 1 inch (2.5 cm) of the lid's side with glue. Fold up the fabric around the side of the lid, slightly pleating the fabric as you go. Repeat all the way around the side.

STEP 6:
Gather together beads from old broken necklaces and pretty buttons off old items of clothing.

STEP 7:
Squeeze a small amount of glue onto the fabric-covered lid of the container and begin sticking on beads and buttons. You can position the beads in a pattern, or place them randomly.

Keep on gluing until the whole lid is thickly covered.

STEP 8:
When the glue is dry, the mini jewelry box is ready to be used. It's perfect for rings and other small items such as earrings.

GLOSSARY

charities (CHER-uh-teez)
Organizations that raise money,
often from donations, and then
use the money to help the needy
or other good causes.

conservation organization
(kon-sur-VAY-shun or-guh-nuh-
ZAY-shun) A group of people
who do work to protect the
natural world from damage
by humans.

costume jewelry
(kos-TOOM JOO-ul-ree)
Jewelry made from inexpensive
materials, such as plastic or glass,
rather than actual gemstones and
precious metals.

environment (en-VY-ern-ment)
The area where plants and
animals live, along with all the
things, such as weather, that
affect that area; often used to
describe the natural world.

environmentally friendly
(in-vy-run-MENT-tul-ee FREND-lee)
Not damaging to the air, land,
rivers, lakes, and oceans, or to
plants and animals.

landfills (LAND-filz)
Large sites where garbage is
dumped and buried.

polluting (puh-LOOT-ing)
Adding damaging substances such as chemicals, gases, or trash to water, land, or air.

profits (PRAH-fits)
Money made by selling something after manufacturing, advertising, and other costs are subtracted from the selling price.

raw materials
(RAW muh-TEER-ee-ulz)
Basic materials, such as rocks, minerals, or trees, that usually come from nature and are used to manufacture a product.

recycled (ree-SY-kuld)
Having to do with used materials turned into new products.

unique (yoo-NEEK)
One of a kind.

upcycling (UP-sy-kling)
Turning an item into something new that has value and is often environmentally friendly.

WEBSITES

Due to the changing nature of Internet links, PowerKids Press has developed an online list of websites related to the subject of this book. This site is updated regularly. Please use this link to access the list:

www.powerkidslinks.com/ftt/jewel/

READ MORE

Di Salle, Rachel, & Ellen Warwick. *Junk Drawer Jewelry*. Kids Can Do It. Toronto: Kids Can Press, 2006.

Kenney, Karen Latchana. *Super Simple Jewelry: Fun and Easy-to-Make Crafts for Kids*. Super Simple Crafts. Minneapolis, MN: Abdo Publishing, 2009.

Senker, Cath. *Fashion Designers*. Celebrity Secrets. New York: PowerKids Press, 2012.

INDEX